MW01284893

ASSAULT
The CRIPPLED CHAMPION
The King Ranch Racehorse

MARJORIE HODGSON PARKER
Illustrated by
CHARLES SHAW

Dedicated to:

Joe, Joanna, Sarah,

And all who hope to run the good race.

With thanks to:

The friendly, helpful people of King Ranch, especially
Helen Kleberg Groves, "Helenita;" Alberto Treviño, "Lolo;" and
Lisa Neely, archivist of the King Ranch Museum. Also, thanks
to my friend Elmer Carter and my mom, Marion Hodgson.

bright sky press
Box 416
Albany, Texas 76430

Library of Congress Cataloging-in-Publication
data in progress.
ISBN 1-931721-34-3 (alk. paper)

Back cover photograph courtesy of the Mr. and Mrs. Robert J. Kleberg, Jr., Collection.

CHAPTER 1

"Try to catch me!" the shiny brown filly teased.

Assault, the colt, turned to see his friend gallop away, her full, dark tail flying behind her. He raced after her, feeling the warm wind, enjoying the sound of their hooves thundering across the pasture. He caught up to her before she reached the big mesquite tree.

"You're so fast!" she said with a soft nicker. "You can catch anyone, can't you?"

"Maybe," he answered, a little shyly.

The two of them bent their necks to nibble the tall, sweet grass in their pasture on King Ranch in South Texas. The morning sun glistened across the dewy range that spread as far as they could see and beyond. Assault was content. Life was good here. It was probably even better for him, he thought, than it was for the mustang horses who used to run here wild and free nearly 100 years ago. It was called the Wild Horse Desert back then.

Assault had heard the older horses talk about it. The stories had passed down through the generations. Before Captain Richard King began King Ranch, very few human beings had lived in the Wild Horse Desert. It was dry, and there was very little water to be had. However, Captain King, a steamboat captain, saw possibilities in the land. On horseback, he discovered a creek, the Santa Gertrudis Creek, which ran through the wilderness. He decided it was a good place to begin a ranch. He planned to dig water wells, improve the land, and stock it with cattle. Beginning in 1853, he bought thousands of acres of that wilderness.

Assault wondered if Captain King had ever caught a mustang to ride on his ranch. He wondered just how fast those free-spirited horses could run.

"I'll bet it was fun to be a mustang," he said, looking over at the filly.

"They were swift, like you," she answered. "I'll bet you would have been the leader."

Assault liked that thought. In King Ranch's wide prairie pastures he loved running with other colts. There were lots of them. He always had the urge to race ahead of them. Almost every time, he could pass them. He liked to be in the lead.

Maybe he would take after his dad. His sire, Bold Venture, was a great racehorse, swift and graceful. Assault's mother, Igual, told him stories about his dad winning important races like the Kentucky Derby. He had won the Derby in 1936, seven years before Assault was born.

As Assault chewed the dewy grass, he imagined that he, too, was a winning racehorse. He pictured his rider, the jockey, wearing a special cap and jacket called silks. King Ranch's silks were brown and white, marked with the Ranch's brand, ᵕᵕᵕ, a "Running W." Assault planned to lift his head high when he carried those colors. He would run like the wind, soaring past other horses and riders and stretching across the finish line.

Assault raised his head now, flaring his nostrils to take in the fresh scent of morning. He imagined the delicious, sweet smell of the winner's blanket of flowers draped over his back as he stood in the winner's circle. Just like his father! Assault wanted to live up to his legacy. And he

wanted to honor Captain King's grandchildren, the Kleberg family, who now ran the ranch.

Assault often saw Robert Kleberg, Jr., "Mr. Bob," who worked closely with the horses and managed the ranch. Assault wanted to make Mr. Bob proud. He wanted to achieve great things for this ranch where he was born.

Just to think about winning made him want to run again.

"'Bye!" he called, as he galloped off and left the filly behind.

A covey of quail fluttered up as he dashed past their hideout. He ran beside the fence that separated his pasture from that of the rich red King Ranch Santa Gertrudis cattle. Assault felt no kinship with them, but he supposed he should be proud of the fact that they were the first American breed of beef cattle. Mr. Bob and his brother Dick had developed the breed to survive in the dry, hot climate.

The Santa Gertrudis cattle seemed snobbish and refused to look at him as he raced by. Assault hoped some day someone would notice how fast he was. He hoped some day he could run in a real race.

He trotted up to his mother. "Did you see me? Did you see me run?" he said, nuzzling her velvety nose.

"Yes. You take after your father," she said. "Listen, my young foal. When you are trained, you can do great things."

"I like to run, Mamma. Running makes my heart happy." He walked around her and ducked his head beneath her to nurse.

"You know, sweet son, one day soon your training will begin. Maybe you'll get to go to the ranch's race rack. But we will not be together anymore then. First, you will leave me for just a few hours a day. Then we'll be apart longer and longer until I'm taken away to another pasture. I won't be with you then. You'll be with the other colts who are growing up—and you will be weaned from me."

Assault stopped nursing. "I don't want to go into training and leave you." His eyes searched her deep, dark ones.

"You are a fine colt, and you will do well," she said. She blew her soft breath on him. "Mr. Bob and all his helpers are kind. I remember when I was a foal, I was very sick. I almost died. They called the King Ranch vet, Dr. Northway to examine me. Mr. Bob's cousin helped Dr. Northway discover what was wrong with me. A hidden infection was making me sick, so the doctor cut it out, and I got well."

Assault leaned against her satiny side. She continued, "Our master, his family and his helpers are your friends. Remember that. You must learn to obey them. If you train and learn the right ways, you can do great things."

"I don't need a master, Mamma. I can do fine by myself. I can run fast. I just need someone to sit on my back in brown and white silks. Don't let them take you away!"

"You'll understand one day. This is the best thing," his mother said in her most comforting nicker. She swished the flies away from him with her tail. "I will always love you. But Mr. Bob can take even better care of you than I can. Besides, you can never win a race if you don't train! You want to be a champion, don't you?"

Assault nodded. Then, weary from running, he lay at his mother's feet, surrounded by yellow and pink wildflowers. He didn't understand what it all meant. As his mother shaded him with her body, he smelled the sweet grass and fell asleep, dreaming of the Kentucky Derby and the blanket of roses.

CHAPTER 2

A few days later, the ranch hands arrived, their brown faces shaded by western hats. The men were called *los Kineños*. *Los Kineños* was a special term in Spanish meaning "the people of King Ranch."

Assault's mother had told him *los Kineños* had come from Mexico when Captain King was first building up the ranch. Most of the families, about 100 people, came from a poor, run-down village called Crullias, Mexico. A terrible drought had killed the crops and grass there. Neither cattle nor people had much to eat. Captain King bought the cattle and planned to fatten them on ranch grass. Since the people needed work, they decided to come across the border to Texas with Captain King, too. From that day on, they lived and worked on the ranch.

Los Kineños had built the first houses and corrals on the ranch. The corrals were made of mesquite posts tied together with wet rawhide, which dried hard, like iron. They dug water tanks and worked for Captain King as cowboys. They introduced the ways of Mexican cowboys, *vaqueros.* One of the *vaqueros'* ideas was using grass ropes to lasso cattle. The Captain used many of their ideas. He took good care of *los Kineños.* Generations later, *los Kineños* were still loyal helpers.

Now they gathered together Assault and his mother, the brown filly and her mother, and the other mares and their foals. They took them to the stable. There, he and his mother were put in their own compartment, a stall. Assault snuffed the air's mixture of smells—men and their sweat, dust, animals, hay. In the stall, someone gave him a breakfast of grain in a feed trough. He put his nose in first to smell it. Delicious! He crunched happily. His mother got some, too. *Los Kineños* came in and petted his mother. She didn't seem afraid, so Assault stood still, too, when they petted him.

He watched *los Kineños* coming and going. Some of the brown-skinned men were old, with sun-baked wrinkles lining their faces. Some were young and strong. They learned from the older ones. Grandfathers and grandsons worked together, side-by-side.

One of *los Kineños* was a dark-eyed boy named Alberto Villa Treviño. His nickname was LoLo. He was thirteen. He took a special liking to Assault and became one of his first teachers. Each morning when the mares and foals came in, he came into Assault's stall. Brushing him and rubbing him with burlap bags, LoLo talked to him.

Assault liked the musical sound of his voice and the scratchy feel of the bags on his reddish-brown coat. After a few days, LoLo put a halter on him. It felt strange, but it didn't hurt. LoLo gave him a good scratch behind the ears when he put it on, and Assault liked that. Sometimes, LoLo pulled a slice of apple from his pocket and fed it to him. Assault sniffed LoLo's pockets, looking for more.

His favorite time was when LoLo washed him with a big soapy sponge and then rinsed him with warm, soothing water. Sometimes he leaned on LoLo and felt the crispness of his starched shirt. Sometimes he nipped at him. He laughed inside when LoLo fussed at him for trying to bite.

Soon LoLo was leading him around by the halter. Day after day, he worked with Assault. He said, "You are a small horse, but you have a big heart and lots of spirit. I've seen you run in the pastures. You're like the wind!" That made Assault feel good.

Many men handled Assault. Some lifted his legs one at a time and cleaned his feet with a hoof pick. Assault spent less time with his mother, and more time with *los Kineños*. He learned to trust them, especially LoLo. He looked forward to the tasty, chewy breakfast each day.

Every afternoon he returned to his pasture. Every morning the routine began again.

Soon, the day came that his mother had warned him about. She wasn't in the pasture to greet him after training. She had been moved. Assault didn't feel ready. He missed her.

Now in the mornings he followed a "bell mare" to the Creek Barn instead of his mother. The bell mare had a bell around her neck. She didn't have a colt of her own, so she acted as a leader to the motherless colts. When her bell went jingling past, the colts fell in line behind her. *Los Kineños* waited for all of them at the barn.

Assault, like the other colts, knew which stall was his to go into for breakfast. He hurried there. It was lonely without his mother, and he was hungry, so he raised his voice with the others, neighing impatiently for food.

LoLo and *los Kineños* were kind and helpful. They seemed to know the colts missed their mothers. They kept Assault and his friends busy. Assault took comfort in remembering that his mother had said: "If you train and learn the right ways, you can do great things."

One fall day when the morning routine was over, Assault ran free, kicking up his heels. He didn't see a surveyor's stake sticking up in the grass. As he galloped, his right, front foot stomped down on the sharp stake. It stabbed through the soft middle part of his hoof, the "frog." It came out the front wall of his hoof. Oh, how it hurt! Assault hobbled around, feeling sick. He wished for his mother.

C H A P T E R   3

As the afternoon sky faded to darkness and the night sounds began, he tried to sleep. The breeze wasn't cold, but Assault felt chilled. He trembled with the pain. His whole leg began aching with pains shooting up from the injury.

The next morning he limped toward the barn for breakfast at the end of the bell mare's line of colts. Usually he trotted near the front of the line. Today, he couldn't keep up. His hoof throbbed! His head pounded.

When *los Kineños* saw him, they called the vet, Dr. Northway, to examine him. Assault was glad his mother had told him about the doctor's gentle care with her. As he was led to an examining room at the barn, he didn't feel afraid of Dr. Northway, but he didn't like the sharp medicine smells.

The doctor examined Assault's hoof. "It's badly injured," he said. The helpers shook their heads sadly. Dr. Northway tried medicines, but Assault didn't feel any better. He heard whispers from some of *los Kineños* that he might never get well. Fear gripped his heart. He knew that sometimes badly injured horses came to this barn and were never seen again.

However, Dr. Northway would not give up. "I'm going to operate and cut out the infected area," he said. "In order to do that, I may have to cut out a big part of his right hoof."

Assault tried not to cause problems as they gave him a shot in his ankle to deaden his foot. Someone held his halter and rubbed his nose as the doctor worked. Assault couldn't feel anything. He didn't look. He just enjoyed the nose rub.

When they were finished, he was taken into a clean stall to rest. As the feeling came back into his foot, it was very sore. He couldn't put any weight on it. Each day for weeks he tried, but it hurt. It seemed better to limp. He limped as LoLo led him. He stumbled a lot.

Some of the other colts snickered at him as they

passed by. "Bet you can't beat us now!" one chestnut-colored colt said, cruelly. Then he tossed his head proudly and trotted away.

"I'll run again, you'll see," Assault called after him. But, secretly, he wondered if he ever would. He wished he could talk to the brown filly. He wondered what she and his other friends were doing.

Assault's days seemed long and boring. He didn't like being penned up and walking instead of running. Even the good breakfast didn't seem exciting. Oh, how he wanted to run!

He knew the colts were playing in the pasture each day. He didn't get to go. Instead, he stood gazing at life passing by, like the sickly horses here, their long faces and pointy ears poking over the stall doors.

LoLo's visits were the best part of the day. LoLo rubbed and brushed him and talked to him. He pulled slices of apple from his pocket and fed them to him one by one. He cleaned his stall and spread a fresh bed of hay. After pouring a helping of grain in the feed trough, LoLo filled the water bucket with cool, sweet water. He put antibiotics on cotton and packed Assault's sore hoof with it.

But one day, LoLo shook his head sadly. "This hoof is not growing as big as your other hooves," he said. "The frog of your foot was badly damaged in the accident, so it's not growing right. And that hoof is as soft as soap! The hoof wall is very thin. How will we ever get a horseshoe on?" LoLo rubbed Assault's ears and stroked his nose. *"No bueno.* Not good." Assault felt too sad even to take a nip at him.

Assault knew a racehorse had to wear shoes. Couldn't anyone help him? Ranch people came in and looked at him and left, puzzled, scratching their heads. What to do? "There's probably no future on the race track for him," someone said darkly.

If it hadn't hurt so badly, Assault would have stomped his foot in anger. He'd never even made it to the track! His head drooped. How could he give up his dream? Was he doomed to be lame? He shivered the flies off his back.

What would his father have done? He thought back to his mother's stories about his dad. Bold Venture had made many sacrifices and suffered many injuries. He had endured pain, learned patience and obedience. Because of injury, he had missed some important races. But once he was well, he put his heart into every race. No matter how far behind he got or how tired he was, Bold Venture had kept trying. He'd lived up to his name.

I'll be like my dad, Assault decided. I will not give up. I will work to get well, work hard. I will keep on until I, too, become a champion! Now, in his heart Assault felt bravery and determination. But in his hoof he felt pain.

CHAPTER 4

When LoLo came to brush him and walk him the next morning, he seemed to sense Assault's determination. As he slowly ran the brush down Assault's back, he said, "You have a heart as big as Texas. I have seen how you keep trying to improve, no matter how injured you are. You won't quit. I can tell you will always do your best." His words encouraged Assault.

Each afternoon, LoLo left to round up cattle with the other cowboys. Now Assault heard LoLo's spurs chink-chink across the hard-packed earth as he walked to the other barn to saddle his quarter horse. Assault knew he'd soon see a cloud of dust as the men rode their horses toward the cattle in far-off pastures.

Assault liked and admired those strong, good-natured, and hard working cow ponies. They were necessary helpers in branding, doctoring, sorting or shipping cattle on the Ranch. Riding the quarter horses, Mr. Bob and *los Kineños* could move the cattle, gather them up, separate them, or rope and hold them.

Although he respected those horses, Assault liked the idea of racing better than chasing cattle. He was glad he was a thoroughbred.

Assault watched some of the younger *Kineños* race home from the little schoolhouse on the ranch. He sniffed at the tired, older *Kineños* who rested in the shade near his stall. He heard the squealing voices of a few small children who played chase nearby. Assault listened as the older *Kineños* shared stories of the past.

One remarked that Captain King had limped. Captain King! Because of the limp, some people had called him *"El Cojo,"* the lame one. People believed that when he was a steamboat captain on the Rio Grande, he had broken his leg, and it never healed right.

"But he was a man of fine character," a wrinkled *Kineño* told the others. "He succeeded in all that he did. The limp never held him back. No matter what happened, it was his habit to look ahead and not backward. This great

Ranch is proof of that—it is famous! It is known as the birthplace of the American ranching industry. We are lucky to be part of King Ranch."

Assault felt lucky, too. He'd always loved his King Ranch home. Hearing the stories, he felt even more proud to be part of it. He resolved more than ever to represent it well and carry its colors. Like the Captain, he would keep pressing on. He would not get discouraged. He would look forward, not back.

After many weeks, he was let out into the pasture. He limped toward the bright green mesquite trees. As the wind tossed the trees' limbs, Assault snatched at the dangling mesquite beans with his teeth. He caught them and ate them one by one. They were some of his favorite things to eat, and somehow it cheered him up.

When he slept, he dreamed of racing and bringing honor to King Ranch.

After a very long time, the soreness went away. Yet, he still protected his hoof. The limp seemed like part of him. He continued his jerky step even as he dreamed of running with the other colts. He wanted desperately to join his friends and to train for racing.

"I will get out there, too," he said to himself. But it seemed that day would never come. He felt very lonely. He whinnied loudly across the wind-waves of prairie grass, wondering if he'd hear a familiar reply. None came.

Then, at last, a bright day dawned. The vet pronounced Assault's foot completely healed. And Dr. Northway solved Assault's shoe problem, too. He designed a special shoe for him. It had a leather pad to cover the damaged frog of his hoof.

However, it was hard to make the shoe stay on his thin hoof. So one talented blacksmith, a farrier, was called in. His specialty was horseshoes. For Assault, he made the shoe turn up at the front where the hoof was thicker. There it could be attached and made to stay on. With this new shoe, Assault felt more hopeful than he had in a long time.

Could he run now? As he was let out to pasture, he decided to try. It was now or never. He sucked in a deep breath and took off. At first he felt a little clumsy. It had been so long! But as he gained speed, his right hoof hit the ground in perfect rhythm with his other hooves. He could do it! He could run! It felt so good!

He stretched his legs out as far as they'd go and thundered across the pasture.

"I can race!" he whinnied into the wind.

CHAPTER 5

By the next fall, when he was stronger and taller, he knew he could hold a rider. He waited impatiently to see what would happen. Would LoLo come take him for real racehorse training?

Finally, one day, LoLo stepped into his stall, slipped a bridle over his head and said, "Time for school!"

Assault rubbed his head against him happily. He was ready.

Perhaps now he could race with a rider! But no. Instead, he had to get used to a saddle on his back. He had to learn to obey LoLo. When LoLo swung up on his back, Assault didn't like it.

He was surprised. His mother never had warned him that he might not like it. He wanted to kick up his heels and buck off LoLo. He fought a little, but since he liked

LoLo, he didn't try too hard to throw him off. He calmed down and began to walk with him.

LoLo was gentle with him as he limped along. And soon Assault felt comfortable with both the saddle and his rider. Maybe this wouldn't be so bad after all. Over the next days in a small corral LoLo taught him to stop, start and turn. Seven or eight horses were getting the same lessons from other *Kineños*.

Finally, LoLo took him out to the ring in the pasture where Assault had seen other horses running in a big circle. Now was his moment. He wondered what it would feel like to run with a rider. Would he stumble?

He didn't have time to worry because right away he felt LoLo's heels press into his sides. Time to go! His muscles tensed, and he broke into a run. It felt as natural as when he used to race the brown filly. In fact, he wanted to run faster, but LoLo kept him under control.

"Bueno!" LoLo cried. "Good!" Feeling light and happy, Assault raised his tail and perked up his ears. His hopes were as high as the wide blue sky.

Every day he ran with LoLo. Every day he grew stronger and faster.

Sometimes as Assault trained, he'd see Mr. Bob watching. His Stetson hat was tilted down to shade his eyes. If dust blew hard, Mr. Bob covered his nose and mouth with the red bandana he wore around his neck. In boots, khaki pants and brown nylon jacket, Mr. Bob did not dress much differently from *los Kineños*. They also wore khaki pants and bandanas. However, Mr. Bob wore a light blue shirt. *Los Kineños* wore khaki shirts and brush jackets to protect them from thorny bushes.

Assault was curious to know if Mr. Bob's pockets held apple slices. He wondered if Mr. Bob was pleased with what he saw when he watched him run.

Mr. Bob seemed to like the way Assault ran because one day LoLo came to take Assault to the ranch's training track. Real race training! Assault felt like prancing for joy. The master believed he could race!

The track was about three miles from his pasture. It was a mile-long oval track, with poles standing along the way to measure distance. As he arrived, Assault heard the deep rumble of a tractor pulling a plow. He watched it as it softened the track's dirt for the horses to run on. Beside the track stood a tall viewing stand. Assault saw some people standing there, peering through binoculars to watch the horses.

The new sounds and smells made him uneasy. The 30 other horses who'd come with him to the track seemed jittery, too.

Soon, however, they all calmed down. Assault was happy to be with the colts that he used to run with. He looked for the filly, but she was not there. She trained at a different time.

Assault knew he was entirely on his own, now. He couldn't depend on his mother or the filly's encouragement. Even worse, he was troubled to find out that the other horses no longer acted friendly. Instead, they just wanted to outrun him.

Only Mr. Bob and his helpers were close to him now. They held his future.

Assault wanted to prove himself quickly. He tried to show off when his turn came to run. But instead of a fast start, he stumbled. The other horses snorted their scorn.

Assault knew he must not let them crush his spirit. Look forward, not back, he reminded himself. The next time he started smoothly.

Some days LoLo rode him. Some days he was ridden by other young *Kineños* who were light-weight and small.

Assault tried to forget his funny foot. He put all his heart into learning to race and obeying the man on his back.

He learned how to start from the gate. He was trained to walk into a narrow entrance, a little stall which had one gate for entering and one for exiting. As he walked in, the back gate was shut behind him. His nose almost touched the front gate which would open at the starter bell.

He didn't mind entering his stall and waiting for the gate to spring open. Some horses did, though, and had to go into their stall backwards. Assault felt like laughing at them, but he didn't let himself.

A man with a stopwatch timed his running and that of the other horses. Assault could feel himself becoming faster. Soon, the ranch's trainer of two-year-old horses, Mr. Egan, put him in a group with the fastest horses.

Running felt so good! Dirt flew into his eyes when he ran behind others. Passing them felt so much better than a face full of dirt.

He spent each night in special stalls near the track where the other racehorses-in-training slept. Each morning, he saw Mr. Bob. Sometimes Mr. Bob was checking the dirt on the track. Sometimes he watched and talked with Trainer Egan and some other "horse people."

The ranch's special trainer, Mr. Max Hirsch, came to watch, too. Assault knew the men must have seen the times he stumbled and limped when he walked or trotted. Would they count that against him? What were they discussing so seriously?

LoLo let him know.

"You're going to South Carolina!" he announced, giving Assault a handful of oats. He seemed thrilled. "You and the fastest horses from the ranch are going on the train. It's good news, boy! Mr. Bob thinks you deserve special training. The trainer is Mr. Max Hirsch. He's the same one who trained your father. He's the best. I'll miss you, *amigo*—my friend. Good luck. Show them your heart for running!"

Assault was excited and a little scared as he was led through the tiny town of Kingsville to the train station. Kingsville had been built on ranch land. When the train was brought to Kingsville, it helped the ranch ship cattle to market. People rode the train in passenger cars, and horses traveled in special boxcars. Assault had heard the lonely cry of the train's whistle carried on the wind across the miles, but he'd never been near a train before.

A crowd of Kingsville people came to watch the horses being loaded onto the train. Assault carefully crossed the ramp from the station platform to the train's boxcar. Inside, the box car was constructed like a little barn, with three stalls on each side facing each other. Each stall held a bucket of water and some hay.

A helper led Assault into his stall and swung the gate shut. The helper stayed in the boxcar to ride with them. In a few minutes, the train started up with a jerk.

Neither Assault nor the other horses liked this strange vehicle that rumbled and shook and felt odd under their feet. The open windows let in lots of noise. But the helper calmed the horses, and soon they were used to the clackety-clack rhythm of the wheels.

Assault began to relax. He was going to Mr. Hirsch, a special racehorse trainer. His dad's trainer! His dream of taking after his father had a chance of coming true after all.

Assault felt thankful. Mr. Bob's confidence in him made him feel more self-assured. Yet, all the way to South Carolina he wondered what this new adventure would be like.

The sun rose and set several times before they finally arrived at the Columbia fairgrounds where his training would take place. Assault was tired of riding. He was turned out into a little pen—nothing like the comforts of King Ranch. In the stable his stall where he slept at night was similar to the one at home, but it didn't smell like home.

Assault felt small compared to the other horses at this place. Now that he was two, he was larger than he'd ever been, but he was not as tall and powerfully built as some of his stable-mates. To appear taller, he held his head high when he walked. Maybe they'd think he was more than 15 hands high.

During training exercises, he tried to ignore the horses' teasing when he stumbled. Several times when he turned around, he nearly fell. Once, he accidentally threw his rider over his head. How embarrassing! What if some day his jockey in the brown and white silks went flying through the air at the racetrack! He put such a thought out of his mind.

He tried not to pay attention when people said, "I don't think he'll ever race with that foot." He heard unkind comments like, "He's ugly. He's scrawny," or "He's not graceful, he's gawky." They'd never said things like that about his father! He could feel his head drooping again.

He wished the brown filly were here to cheer him up. He wished he had a friend to stand head to tail with to swish away the flies. He wished for mesquite beans to chew. He missed the familiar, kind hands of LoLo and his encouraging words. He missed King Ranch.

S uddenly, he yanked his head up and shook his mane. What was he saying? He shuddered away the flies, along with the dreary thoughts. Unkind words were not going to defeat him. They were like flies biting, pestering him. He would swish them away.

Mr. Bob knew better than anyone else, and he believed in him. Assault would honor King Ranch! He would give his whole heart to being the best he could be. He'd show them!

One day, he heard Mr. Hirsch defend him to the people who said mean things. He said, "When he walks or trots, it looks as if he's going to fall down. But he gallops true. There isn't a thing wrong with his action when he runs." Assault's heart felt much lighter after that.

Each day he worked hard to do everything his trainers said. The days started very early with grooms turning on

the stable lights and saying, "Good morning! It's 4:30 a.m. and time for breakfast."

Sometimes, before the grooms came in, Mr. Hirsch came by to look at all the horses.

By the time he left, Assault was really hungry.

Once breakfast was over, Assault enjoyed the groom's scratchy brush. Even before the sun peeked up and the sky blushed pink, Assault was groomed and saddled and ready to go. He and the other horses were lined up in an orderly manner and walked to the track. Assault liked the firm sand on the track. It was easy on his feet.

Mr. Hirsch walked behind the horses. Sometimes Mr. Bob visited from Texas, bringing his wife, Helen, and their daughter, whom they called *Helenita*, "little Helen." They would walk with Mr. Hirsch. Sometimes boys would travel from the Ranch to ride the horses. Assault liked the familiar smell of his ranch people.

Each morning Mr. Hirsch stood out on the track with his stopwatch and white handkerchief. He timed the horses as they ran. Assault soon learned his jockey was watching Mr. Hirsch. When the handkerchief waved one way, his rider would let Assault run faster. When the handkerchief went up and down, the jockey would slow Assault down. Assault always liked it best when the handkerchief said "faster!"

Sometimes Assault ran short distances, sometimes long. At first, he was ridden at an easy gallop. About once a week, the pace was quickened. After he got in shape, he was ready to run really fast.

Every day about mid-morning when his routine was over, he was "cooled out" by his groom walking him. Then he lined up with the other horses in front of Mr. Hirsch. Mr. Hirsch checked each horse's legs.

After that, Assault was taken into the barn and bathed. He stood still while the groom, using a hoof pick, picked rocks and dirt out of his hooves. Next, he wiped Assault's nostrils free of dust. If the dust had been bad, the groom would give him eye drops. Assault liked to try to bite the groom with the eye drops.

When a sheet was draped over him, Assault knew it was time to walk with the groom along the shed row, a porch-like area that ran the length of the stables. Afterward he got a morning treat in a sunny little paddock. Since the paddock had little grass, a helper mowed grass in a nearby field. He fed the freshly cut grass to the horses. It tasted good, but not as good as ranch grass.

After lunch Assault was ready for his nap. He felt relaxed after the groom had rubbed his legs with liniment. It was soothing to have his tired legs stroked. On days when he had a hard workout, his legs were covered with Mr. Hirsch's special "mud formula" to take any soreness out. The groom put clay in his hooves, too, to keep them from aching. He then wrapped brown paper or newspaper around Assault's legs and feet. By the time the quilted cotton bandage was pinned on, Assault felt his eyes closing in sleep. The rest of the day he took it easy.

Although he ate lots of grain and grass, he still didn't grow as tall or heavy as the other two-year-olds. Standing or walking beside them still made him feel gawky. But he was learning more every day. The more he ran, the more his confidence grew. He stumbled less.

His funny hoof got very special attention. Mr. Hirsch gave Assault his own personal farrier, named John. Farrier John was the only one allowed to work with Assault so that his shoes would fit perfectly. Assault stood very still while Farrier John worked. He knew better than to bite him!

CHAPTER 8

One day in June of 1945, Assault was loaded onto a train and taken to his first race at Belmont Park in New York. His whole body quivered with excitement.

At the track, he was given a number and a jockey in brown and white silks. He couldn't believe it. A real race! This was his moment!

With the other horses, he paraded past the grandstand where people sat all dressed up. The men's suits and hats were nothing like the western hats and clothes of his ranch people. The ladies wore dresses, gloves and their own style of bright hats.

Assault felt specially dressed, too, with a number cloth under his saddle and a jockey on his back. He wore his own sort of "hat" as well, a hood with holes for his eyes and ears. The hood shielded his face from flying dirt clods kicked up by the running horses in front of him. His jockey wore goggles for protection. Assault hoped to dash ahead early in the race, so that neither he nor his jockey would feel any dirt. He expected to fly as fast as New York's silvery seagulls that winged down the track.

He entered his stall in the starting gate. So far, except for the crowd watching, it was just like practice. Some of the more nervous horses were being rowdy, though, and thrashing around in the gate. For each of the wild ones, a man stood on a little ledge inside that horse's stall to help calm him. Sometimes a man would raise a horse's tail so the horse wouldn't sit down. Sometimes he'd hold a horse's head firmly to keep him from tossing it wildly from side to side.

Assault didn't need anyone to calm him. He just wanted to run!

As everyone settled down, the bell rang. The gates flew open. Assault lunged out of his gate as he heard the track announcer shout, "They're off!"

He wanted to run fast from the start. But the jockey held him back, saving Assault's energy. Assault was used to that from training. He had to obey. Still, he hated to fall behind. He didn't like dirt flying in his face. He knew at some point the jockey would give him his head—would let him run his fastest. When would that be?

He swiveled his ears and heard the pounding hooves around and behind him. He saw the flying tails and blur of colors of the horses and jockeys ahead of him. He smelled the flying dirt. He passed poles along the track that marked the distance they'd run. How many poles would he pass before his moment finally came?

At last, Assault's rider gave him full rein, asking for his all. Assault gladly gave it everything he had. He laid his ears back and ran with a huge burst of energy. But it wasn't enough. Even though he passed several horses, he was too far behind to catch the lead horses.

When he crossed the finish line, he was in twelfth place. Assault was humiliated. He had failed.

The jockey, however, was kind to him. He patted Assault's hot neck and said, "Good boy. You did well for your first race." Assault wanted to tell him he could do much better than that. Next time he would win first place!

But he didn't.

Finally in his fourth start in July, he could feel

himself edging ahead of the other horses, just like in the old days at the ranch. Heart pounding, he raced on, urged on by his jockey.

And he won!

He wanted to kick up his heels in glee. Instead, he walked with dignity, like the other winners he'd watched.

Things would be different from now on. He was sure this was the beginning of a winning streak.

Yet, it was not to be. In nine races, he won only once more.

Each time the groom or "hot walker" walked him, to cool him down after a race, Assault would try to relax. As he drank a few swallows of cool water and then walked more, he'd make an effort to forget his fears about the future. As he was bathed, he'd try to enjoy it as the warmish water and soft, soapy sponge soothed him.

But he couldn't fully relax, because he remembered what his mother had told him. She had said a horse's performance as a two-year-old was all-important. If he did well, he could be entered in the important three-year-old races like the Kentucky Derby. If not …

He knew winning only two races wasn't good enough. Someone had said he was "just better than an empty stall." No one thought he was fast. No reporters took his picture. No one called him "a favorite."

What did Mr. Bob think? That was the most important question. He saw Mr. Bob at the races. There, Mr. Bob was not dressed in khakis. He wore a double-breasted suit and hat called a fedora. Mr. Bob's family came, too. Helen and Helenita wore flowered dresses and gloves and, sometimes, hats. They smelled sweet when they petted him.

Assault knew they all cheered for him, no matter what. That helped. Yet, he wondered …

After a race, he often saw Mr. Bob talking seriously with trainers or riders. What was he saying? Did he still believe Assault could be a champion? Would he enter him in next year's races or ship him home in defeat?

Discouraged, Assault waited to see what would happen after racing season. No one had said anything. Where would he spend the winter?

CHAPTER 9

When he boarded the train, he heard that it was bound for the Columbia, South Carolina, training facility. South Carolina, not Texas! That meant Mr. Bob thought Assault had run well enough to try again.

Although he missed Texas, Assault was glad to be back at the training grounds. He frolicked in the paddock and chased the cooling wind in its small space. He had a second chance! He would train even harder, eat more and grow stronger.

The stable hands took good care of him. They kept him warm, well fed and exercised. They laughed sometimes, because he ate so much. When the wind blew its coldest, they came in saying, "Happy New Year" to him and to each other. "Happy 1946!"

A groom gave Assault a handful of oats and said, "Happy

birthday to you, old boy. Today, you are legally a three-year-old thoroughbred. This can be a big year for you!" Assault's ears perked up. Spring would bring all the big races!

As the days grew warmer, Assault was up long before the barn rooster, feeling frisky and happy. He worked hard. He stumbled less. Although South Carolina still didn't feel like home, he grew to like Mr. Hirsch and Farrier John and the jockeys and grooms. He was always glad to see Mr. Bob when he visited.

He could sense everyone's excitement about the racing season. He listened to their lively talk. Energy was in the air.

This year, he felt wiser and more confident. He had a better understanding of men and other horses. So when he entered the starting gate for his first race as a three-year-old, he knew he was going to make the most of this chance.

And he did. He won!

The thrill of it was as great as his very first win. The cheers, the cameras and commotion added to his excitement. It was hard to settle down, even after his jockey loped him slowly around the track to cool down.

In his second race, the Wood Memorial, he won again. Surprising everyone, he beat a favored horse. More importantly, that win meant he could run in the Kentucky Derby. Assault's hopes soared. Suddenly news reporters were swarming around his stall. Flash bulbs popped. Someone called him "the Club-footed Comet." Another dubbed him "the Texas Terror." The reporters asked Mr. Hirsch about Assault's right hoof.

"One bad blacksmith might put Assault out of racing for months or even forever," Mr. Hirsch said. Assault was glad to have Farrier John. John traveled all over the country with him. No one wanted anything to go wrong with that foot again!

In May when Assault traveled by train to a race, he knew where he was going. The stable hands had been talking about it all month: May 4, 1946, was Kentucky Derby Day. It was the day he'd dreamed of since he was a foal. He was going to run the same race his father had won.

A few days before the race, he arrived at the famous track, Churchill Downs, in Louisville, Kentucky. He snuffed the wind excitedly. It smelled sweet with blooming dogwood trees and yellow forsythia bushes and bright flowers. This race was called the "Run for the Roses." Assault had dreamed about the beautiful garland of fresh roses, which would be draped over the neck of the winning horse. He wanted to smell the roses!

The barn swallows chattered happily as he was led into his stall. Now he smelled liniment and coffee and horses and humans. He wasn't sure if he could sleep, but he knew he needed to rest. He'd never run a race as long as the Kentucky Derby. It was one and one-fourth miles long.

The morning of May 4 was rainy. He was up long before daylight. He enjoyed some sweetened oats, but he wasn't fed his usual feed. On race day, he always ate lightly. As he worked with his exerciser and trainer and got familiar with the track, he felt full of energy. What would this day be like? Who would be running?

Assault had heard a lot about Lord Boswell of Maine Chance Farm, a horse that was everyone's favorite. Assault wasn't sure who he was. But later that day, as all the horses and riders milled around in the paddock before the race, he saw him. Lord Boswell was a tall, strong, beautiful thoroughbred. He looked confident and haughty. Assault wanted to bite him.

Assault felt very small, but, he told himself his heart was every bit as big as Lord Boswell's. Maybe even bigger.

No one could see hearts, after all. And Assault planned to run with all of his.

In the paddock, Mr. Bob, Mr. Hirsch and others came for Assault's saddling. They wished luck to each other and Assault's young jockey, Warren Mehrtens. They petted Assault and wished him luck, too. Mr. Hirsch quietly gave Warren some special instructions for the race. Assault couldn't hear them, but he was prepared to obey whatever Warren guided him to do.

Assault stood still as the groom draped the cloth with his number over his back, then placed the saddle over it. The groom passed the wide girth strap under Assault's belly. Then he tightened it along with another thinner strap that went over the saddle. With his hands, he stretched Assault's front legs to loosen any muscle or skin that might have been pinched in the straps.

Assault shuffled his feet and tossed his head. He was ready to run!

At last the paddock judge said, "Riders up!" Mr. Hirsch cupped his hands and boosted Warren, the jockey, into the saddle. Horses and riders went out onto the track. Assault was close to Lord Boswell, so he held his head high.

Flapping flags caught the moist wind, and Assault breathed deeply. He decided to enjoy every moment of this big day. As he paraded out to the starting gate, he heard a band playing. The air seemed charged with excited energy. He admired the lush green grass and white wooden fences that surrounded the freshly softened track.

On the inside of the track's oval, a fenced-in, grassy area called the infield was teeming with people. Assault gazed toward the outside of the track at the famous old wooden grandstand which was packed with people. Its roof was crowned with two round towers with pointed tops, the Twin Spires.

The stand held three tall levels of brightly dressed people, and they were all singing! People in the infield were singing, too. Thousands of voices sang "My Old Kentucky Home." Assault felt the enthusiasm and happiness of the crowd.

Even nature smiled with bright tulips and crocus. Assault sniffed the blending of smells—perfumes, flowers, concession food, people and animals. He enjoyed the reds, greens, yellows and blues of the jockeys' silks. Best of all, he liked carrying his rider in the brown and white silks.

Assault studied the men and women in the crowd squeezing up to the fence as he walked by. Men were dressed in military uniforms or suits. The ladies were brightly dressed, and their big flowered and feathered straw hats looked good enough to eat! A young boy peeking from around his father's legs called out, "Hello, horsies."

Suddenly, Assault heard Lord Boswell snort at him. "We'll see if you're really 'the club-footed comet,'" he said.

CHAPTER 10

A ssault made no answer. He intended to beat all the horses, but now he especially wanted to leave Lord Boswell in the dust.

He hoped his jockey Warren knew what to do to win. Like Assault, Warren had never been in the Kentucky Derby. Assault could sense his rider's nervous energy.

To warm up, the horses and riders passed the starting gate, going up and around the far turn. They walked, loped and galloped, then turned around and headed back to the starting gate for the race. Each horse was assigned a man to lead him into the gate.

Assault entered. As he was closed into his narrow stall in the gate, his nose touched the cool iron front. His sides nearly touched the gate walls. Assault was ready. His legs quivered with excitement. He felt Warren tighten and grab firmly onto his mane. He knew Warren would hold on to it to keep from losing his balance when Assault suddenly bolted out the gate. Warren then would let go of the mane and hold only the reins.

Because a jockey's stirrups were so high, Assault knew Warren couldn't squeeze with his knees for balance. He knew jockeys had to ride differently from LoLo and the ranch's cowboys who pressed with their legs for steadiness. Jockeys balanced on a horse's back using only the reins and their skill.

A man called the "starter" stood on a tall perch in front and to the side of the gates. The starter waited for all 17 horses to get loaded and ready. Assault was impatient. Why didn't those nervous horses stop stomping and rearing and settle down? The men who had led them into their stalls tried hard to hold the horses still.

Suddenly, the starter jangled a bell, and the gates sprang open. A loud announcer cried, "They're off!" Assault's heart hammered as he leapt out for a good start.

Several horses shot ahead, angling for the inside lane. Assault wanted to race past them. Warren was holding him back. Still in fifth place at the first turn, Assault wondered if Warren knew what he was doing.

Steadily, Assault moved up to third, still waiting for Warren to ask for his best run. He had been trained to wait, to obey, but it was so hard to do!

At last, Warren moved his hands and body forward on Assault's neck and made a smooching sound. Assault knew that meant, "Run as hard as you can."

Assault gave it all he had for the final stretch. Every muscle worked its hardest. He extended his body as far as it would go, as if reaching for the finish line. He felt Warren stretching forward, too. It felt as if Warren's body were a part of his own.

The roar of the crowd swelled above the thundering hooves around him. He passed the two horses in front of him, just like he used to do at the ranch. Suddenly he could hear nothing except his own hard breath and hooves pounding near him. Where was Lord Boswell?

He didn't dare look back. He charged straight ahead toward the finish line. He seemed to be flying. In seconds he was there. He streaked across it ahead of all the others. "Eight lengths ahead," the announcer said! He couldn't believe it. He had won the Kentucky Derby!

Warren was praising him; the announcer was shouting his name. But the surprised crowd wasn't cheering very loudly. He knew they had thought Lord Boswell would win. Their disappointed applause was only polite. Assault didn't mind. He knew Mr. Bob and his ranch friends were delighted and cheering loudly. Assault thought his heart would burst with the thrill of it all. He had proved his master right and made him proud. He had brought honor to King Ranch!

Assault held his head high as he pranced with his jockey into the Churchill Downs winner's circle. In the infield he stood in the grass center of a horseshoe-shaped border of red and yellow flowers. White fence, clapping people and more planted flowers surrounded him. The noisy crowds in the stands looked on.

It was just like his dream: his rider in the brown and white silks, the delicious smelling blanket of roses draped over his shoulders. Warren was handed a huge bouquet of roses, too. Cameras clicked. Ranch friends stroked his nose. The trophy gleamed as it was handed to Mr. Bob. Assault wished his mother, the filly and LoLo could see him now.

After he was washed, fed, and put up for the night on a comfortable bed of fresh straw, Assault realized Lord Boswell had not even placed in the race. He wondered how he could have outrun that bigger, stronger horse.

He heard the grooms and jockeys talking. Now that Assault had won the Kentucky Derby, two other very important races would follow: the Preakness Stakes and the Belmont Stakes. And he would face Lord Boswell again.

If Assault won both races, he'd win the Triple Crown title. No horse born in Texas had won it. Only six horses in 70 years of racing history had won the three races. Yet Mr. Bob seemed to think Assault could do it.

Assault's dream grew larger to match Mr. Bob's. Could he make history for King Ranch?

Then, he began to worry again. The old voices of doubt haunted him. He still limped when he walked. He still wasn't powerfully built. Maybe this win had been only luck. In the next race when he met Lord Boswell again it would take more than luck.

He'd overheard jockeys and trainers planning before races. A jockey had to be wise and know just what to do—when to let his horse push through a gap between horses, when to hold back. A jockey had to stay perfectly balanced in the saddle and understand his horse well enough to know just how to encourage him. A jockey had to study the other horses in a race, too, to see how they performed. Then, he'd figure out how best to beat them.

By the next race, Lord Boswell's jockey would know better how to beat Assault. And Lord Boswell's rippling muscles would be ready to power him ahead. Assault would have to run faster than ever. He would have to sense exactly what his jockey wanted. Assault was too tired to think about it now, so he fell asleep dreaming of the Triple Crown.

The next race toward the Triple Crown was in just one week. This one was the Preakness Stakes. For the first time in his life, Assault was the favorite for a race. His father, Bold Venture, had won the Preakness, too. That would make it mean even more if he won.

CHAPTER 11

The Preakness was held at Pimlico Race Course in Baltimore, Maryland. He arrived by train a few days in advance. As Assault worked out, he saw the grandstands and Pimlico's big, yellow Victorian clubhouse. With white trim, green shutters, and a big wrap-around porch, it stood elegantly beside the track. On top of the clubhouse, a weather vane in the shape of a horse and rider swiveled in the wind.

The grooms said after the race, according to tradition, the weather vane would be re-painted with the colors of the winner's silks. Assault hoped the weather vane would be brown and white before the end of race day.

On the day of the race, Assault rested his bad foot in a wooden tub of ice. It felt very cold, but he didn't mind. Sometimes running made his foot ache, and ice

took the ache away. He had to feel and run his best because Lord Boswell and his rider would not be taken by surprise again.

After the paddock saddling, with Warren on his back, Assault "paraded to the post," the starting gate. He passed the old clubhouse, where people packed the porch to watch, and continued past the grandstands to the gate.

After warming up, Assault lined up with the nine other horses in the gate. His heart beat fast. His feet fidgeted. He knew the gate would spring open any second. He felt Warren ready himself.

As the bell clanged, Assault burst out the open gate for a good start. In the first part of the race, another horse veered to the rail in front of him, slowing him. Assault felt Warren release him to run faster and get back his position.

Warren was letting him go swiftly earlier than he had in the Derby. Assault happily forged to the front. It was great not to be held back. It felt good to run hard.

In the final stretch of the race, however, Assault felt something was wrong. He was getting tired! This was the moment he needed more energy, not less! The others were catching up.

He twisted his ears to hear the pounding hooves closing in on him in the final stretch. He heard the horses' hard breathing getting closer. He could almost feel the hot breath.

Out of the corner of his eye, he saw a horse drawing up beside him. It was Lord Boswell! Assault's mouth frothed, his lungs ached. He couldn't let Lord Boswell pull ahead!

He felt the sting of his rider's whip. Assault tried, tried, but he couldn't run any faster. His legs felt very heavy.

Warren didn't whip him again. He seemed to know Assault didn't need it. Warren stretched over Assault's neck, urging him on with his body and his voice. Assault's body wanted to give up, but his heart drove him onward. The finish line was close. If he could just hang on! He gave it everything he had.

He won by a neck!

As Warren slowed him to a walk and let him cool down, Assault's heart pounded hard. His breath came in great heaves. He'd never felt quite like this at the end of a race.

Exhausted but victorious, he entered the winner's circle. He enjoyed the coolness of the flower-blanket of black-eyed Susans, Maryland's state flower, as it was draped over his shoulders. The crowds and his ranch people milled around him as his tired, happy heart slowed.

Although he had won, he didn't hear the excited praise from reporters that he expected. He heard something else: voices doubting him. They said the distance had been too much for him. He'd been losing ground at the end of the race. He hadn't finished strong.

A reporter called him "scrawny" again. What happened to the names he liked, such as the Chocolate Champ or the Texas Terror? No one called him that this time.

The next race, the Belmont Stakes, was longer. In fact, it was nicknamed "the Test of the Champion," because so many horses tired out before they could finish it. Only the strongest could make it.

The fans decided Assault might not last the distance. He was dropped from the favorite spot for the final race for the Triple Crown. They rated him behind Lord Boswell again.

Assault was learning not to listen to the fickle fans. He would listen only to Mr. Bob who believed in him. That's the hope he took with him to Belmont Park in New York for the third and final race for the Triple Crown.

After three weeks of resting and preparing, he was more determined than ever. He knew that finishing even a fraction of an inch behind another would make him one of the many who *almost* won the crown. He couldn't let that happen. He wouldn't!

As Assault was saddled under the big trees in the paddock at Belmont, people gathered around. He'd never been in a paddock with such a crowd of people. They seemed as excited as he was. When they talked, their words sounded peculiar to him. Their accent sounded nothing like the slow drawl of his ranch people.

Trying to relax, he gazed at the flowers and the shady lawn. They looked delicious, but he was only hungry for a win.

As Warren was boosted up onto the saddle, Assault felt

calmed by his rider-friend's familiar weight. A sudden, long trumpet blast startled him. It was a signal meaning "last call to the post."

As part of the ceremony, a red-jacketed rider led Assault and Warren and the other horses and riders up the clay ramp onto the track. As they slowly paraded to the post, Assault gazed at the blue lakes in the infield. Flags flapped, and people clapped.

Things were familiar here. His very first race had been here, he remembered. He had run poorly then. Surely that wouldn't happen again. Even though he still limped when he walked, he stumbled much less now than he did then. He was a winner now. He reminded himself to act like Captain King and look forward, not back.

He let go of his worries as he warmed up by walking, jogging and galloping along the freshly plowed, sandy track. It felt good to his feet.

After warm-up, the seven horses lined up in the long, white starting gate. Assault was tense. He could tell some of the other horses were especially nervous. Lord Boswell, however, seemed very confident. He looked like a mighty mass of pent-up power. He glanced over at Assault and snorted.

Assault felt sweat beading up on his neck. He shuffled his feet. Suddenly, the bell clanged, and the gates sprang open.

With his head bowed and knees bent, Assault thrust himself forward eagerly. Then he stumbled! That foot again!

Assault felt Warren struggle to keep his balance. He heard the audience gasp. He saw the other horses dash ahead.

Almost instantly, Warren re-gained his balance and steadied Assault. As Assault fought to recover his running rhythm, he wondered if he'd already lost the race. A good start was essential, and he was behind. Without this win, there'd be no Triple Crown.

He responded eagerly as Warren led him to the inside lane. Warren's firm balance and confidence helped Assault re-gain speed. He quickly moved up. He even passed Lord Boswell! Yet, by the mile pole, he was still in fourth place.

He had plenty of energy to run faster. He waited for Warren to let him go, but he kept holding Assault back, holding him back. Was Warren remembering the last race when he'd let Assault run fast too early? Was he now being too careful? Would he wait too long?

Assault knew he had to obey. Mr. Bob had chosen Warren for a reason. To the rhythm of his running hooves, Assault chanted to himself, "Run hard for the master. Run hard for King Ranch."

At last, in the long final stretch to the finish line, Warren let him go. Assault pinned his ears back and exploded forward with everything he had. Warren leaned frontward like a part of him, coaxing him on.

The thundering hooves of the three horses ahead of him filled his ears. Breath came in gasps. Dirt flew behind the horses' hurrying hooves and hit him in the face. He ran hard.

He was catching up! His mouth frothed. As he passed, other horses' froth blew back at him. Every horse was straining as hard as he could.

Assault exerted all he had to pull ahead. If he could just keep running … Just a little farther … He gave it his whole heart. This is what he was born to do!

As Assault streaked across the finish line, the announcer's voice shouted that he had won by three lengths.

He had done it! He had won the Belmont Stakes and the Triple Crown!

Assault heard Warren whoop his excitement. As Warren patted Assault and walked him around to cool off, Assault pranced in celebration. Now he wasn't just "a horse with a gimp leg." He was a champion!

Warren galloped him back to the finish line and paused. Assault stood still as Warren, with his whip raised, saluted to a race official called a steward. It was a part of the ceremony after the race.

Warren rode Assault into the infield's half circle of green shrubbery—the winner's circle. The gleaming Belmont trophy with its sleek silver horses was displayed on a cloth-covered table. It caught the sunlight and flashed it back.

CHAPTER 13

Assault delighted in the chattering reporters surrounding him, squatting close to take pictures. He felt so frisky he wanted to nip a reporter just to see him jump. But he didn't.

Assault breathed in deeply, gratefully. He liked the spicy scent of the white carnations they draped over him. He heard the applause—loud and thunderous this time.

In all the excitement, though, nothing felt as good as his master's touch. Bob Kleberg walked up to Assault and smiled, stroking Assault's sweaty neck.

"Well done," he said proudly.

Assault stood nobly by the man who'd believed in him. Mr. Bob was handed the trophy as cameras clicked. Talk swirled. People praised Mr. Bob and Assault. Helen and Helenita smiled.

The reporters nicknamed Assault the Chocolate Soldier, "the horse who ran on three hooves and a heart." They declared he was the first Texas-bred horse to win the Triple Crown, and it was a crown indeed for one of America's largest ranches, King Ranch.

Assault hoped one day he'd have a chance to tell his mother and the brown filly what this great day had been like. He knew at the moment, LoLo, *los Kineños* and other ranch friends were celebrating the news in Texas. Assault hoped his success would inspire LoLo to continue his kindness to other young horses. He hoped his story would encourage every colt with a dream.

His mother had been right. The master had known best. He'd had looked past Assault's limp and seen his promise. Now Assault was the Triple Crown Champion. Against all odds, he had run and won.

Assault went on to win 18 important races and $674,720 in his career. The year he won the Triple Crown, he was elected Horse of the Year. At one point, Assault had earned more money by winning races than any other horse in the world. Only 11 horses in history have won the Triple Crown.

Assault never sired a thoroughbred colt. In 1950, he was retired to the King Ranch pastures he loved. He lived out his remaining 21 years at home with his friends on the 825,000 acre ranch. He was a favorite of many King Ranch visitors. During that time, Dr. Northway wrote, "He is quite a pet to all of the owners and to all who know him ... this grand old champion horse."

When Assault died at age 28, Dr. Northway and Assault's Kineño friends spoke at his funeral. A Texas granite slab marks the place he is buried on the King Ranch.

On the 50th anniversary of Assault's win, a celebration was held at the King Ranch Museum. It was attended by people from across the country who were connected with Assault's life. Many stories were told about this famous horse, who is still remembered for having brought honor to Texas with his courage and endurance.